FRANKENSTEIN; OR THE MAN AND THE MONSTER!

H. M. MILNER

FRANKENSTEIN; OR, THE MAN AND THE MONSTER!

Table of Contents

FRANKENSTEIN; OR, THE MAN AND THE MONSTER!

H. M. MILNER

Kessinger Publishing reprints thousands of hard−to−find books!

Visit us at http://www.kessinger.net

_____

A PECULIAR ROMANTIC, MELO−DRAMATIC PANTOMIMIC SPECTACLE, IN

FRANKENSTEIN; OR, THE MAN AND THE MONSTER!

TWO ACTS. Founded principally on Mrs. Shelly's singular Work, entitled, FRANKENSTEIN; OR, THE MODERN PROMETHEUS; and partly on the French Piece, "Le Magicien et le Monstre."

```
DRAMATIS PERSONAE.
PRINCE DEL PIOMBINO
FRANKENSTEIN
RITZBERG
QUADRO
STRUTT
JULIO
(* * * * * *)
ROSAURA
EMMELINE
LlSETTA
Nobles, Guards, and Attendants on the Prince, Peasants, c.
```

SCENE – The Estate of the Prince del Piombino near the foot of Mount Etna.
TIME – From Sunset on one day, till Midnight the next.

THE FATE OF

FRANKENSTEIN

ACT I.

SCENE I.

The Gardens of the Prince del Piombino's Villa. — At the back a River, beyond which, Picturesque Country. On the P. S. side, the Entrance to the Villa. On the O.P. side, a small Pavilion.)

Enter QUADRO, STRUTT, *and* LISETTA, *from the villa, meeting male and female Villagers.*

Lis. And you think yourself a vastly great man, Mr. Strutt, I suppose.

Strutt. Philosophers are not content with thinking, I know it. My master's a great man, and I'm like the moon to the sun, I shine with a reflected brightness.

Quad. Great man, indeed! I should like to know what there is great about either of you. A couple of adventurers, whom my poor silly dupe of a master, (Heaven help him!) has brought from that beggarly place, Germany; and I suppose you'll never leave him whilst he has got a ducat.

Strutt. Pooh! for his ducats! we want his ducats, indeed! when we could make gold out of any rubbish; your worthless head for instance, Signor Quadro. My master is the most profound philosopher, and consequently the greatest man that ever lived; to tell you what he can do is impossible; but what he cannot do, it would be still more difficult to mention.

Quad. Yes, his way of making gold, I fancy, is by conveying it out of other people's pockets. He may make gold, but he'd much rather have it made to his hand, I've a notion.

Strutt. Signor Quadro, it is fortunate for you that my master does not hear you, and that (Considering the choice bottles of Catanian wine that you have from time to time been

3

pleased to open for me) I'm too discreet to tell him; — for, oh! signor Quadro, his power is terrible; — he could prevent you from ever passing a quiet night again!

Quad. When I've got three quarts of good Rhenish in my skin, I'll give him leave, if he can. Your master is a water–drinker, sir, he keeps no butler; I never knew any good of a man that drank water and kept no butler.

Strutt. At all events, master Quadro, that's an offence which you cannot lay to my charge; I have the most philosophical principles upon the subject; — I drink water, Signor Quadro, only when I can't get any thing better.

Quad. And that's generally the case, I fancy, when you can't find some good–natured simpleton, like the Prince del Piombino, to keep you and your master together. Instead of board–wages, he billets you upon the kitchen of any body that's fool enough to take you into it.

Strutt. Be assured of this, Signor Quadro, I am not ungrateful; when any kind friend has the goodness to take me in, I do the best in my power to return the compliment

Quad. The devil doubt you.

Strutt. But for my master, signor Quadro, don't think that all the wine in Sicily is any object to him, he could turn that river into wine if he thought proper, — I've seen him do it, sir, and convert a quart of simple water into a bottle of prime Burgundy.

Quad. Can he? Can he do that? Then he has an easy way of making me his sworn friend for life. Only let him turn — I won't be unreasonable; I won't say a word about the river — only let him turn the pump in our stable–yard into a fountain of claret, and I'll never purloin another bottle of my master's, so long as I'm a butler.

Lis. And pray, Mr. Strutt, has all this philosophy and learning quite driven the thoughts of love out of your head? I suppose you fancy yourself now quite above us poor weak women?

Strutt. Not at all, my dear creature; for the man who has the Impudence to fancy himself above the fairest half of human nature has sunk immeasurably below it.

4

FRANKENSTEIN; OR, THE MAN AND THE MONSTER!

Quad. Egad! philosophy has not made quite a tool of the fellow. But pray now, my good Mr. Strutt, amongst all this transmuting of metal, and converting of water, can you inform us what it is that this wonderful master of yours is doing in that pavilion, where he remains constantly shut up, day and night, and into which no mortal but himself is ever permitted to penetrate?

Strutt. You would like to know, would you?

Quad. Yes I should, very much indeed.

Lis. Oh yes, I'd give the world to know, I should so like to find out the secret.

Strutt. (after a pause) And so should I.

Quad. What then, you can't tell us?

Lis. Or perhaps you won't.

Strutt. Why you see — I'm not exactly certain — but I partly guess — (they cling to him with eager curiosity)–that is, I suspect — that it is — something that will astonish your weak nerves, one day or another.

Quad. Pshaw!

Lis. A nasty, ill–natured fellow — see how I'll serve you, the next time you try to kiss me. (music without.

Quad. But hark! his highness approaches with his lovely sister, the lady Rosaura. Back! back! all of you, show him proper respect.

(They are joined by other domestics, male and female, who form in order. A Gondola approaches the shore, from which the Prince, Rosaura *, and* Attendants *land. As the* Prince *advances, all salute him.)*

Prince. Enough, enough, my friends, hasten to the villa, and busy yourselves in preparations for the festival I wish to give in honour of the illustrious genius, who honours my house with his presence.

Quad. (aside) A festival, too! for a man who drinks no wine. Well, there's one consolation; there'll be more for those who do — and I'll do my best to make up for his deficiencies, he may depend on't.

Strutt. (to Lis.) If there's dancing, may I claim the honour — ?

Lis. Will you try to find out your master's secret for me? —

Strutt. It is positively against his orders, to pry into his concerns — and do you know, there is but one person in the world whose commands could induce me to disobey those of my master.

Lis. And who may that be, pray?

Strutt. My mistress, you jade. *(takes her under his arm, and exeunt with Quadro, Domestics, into the Palace.)*

Prince. I feel most deeply that rank and opulence can never do themselves greater honour, than by protecting and assisting talent and genius.

Ros. And never, surely, did genius clothe itself in a more enviable guise, than in the person of Frankenstein. How different is the unassuming modesty of his demeanour, his winning gentleness, from the harsh pedantry and formal solemnity of schoolmen in general.

Prince. Theirs is the solemn mockery of mere pretension, which genius, such as Frankenstein's, despises. — The universities of Germany have all bent to his prodigious talent, and acknowledged his superiority:– the prince who, conscious of his merit, rewards, assists, and forwards it, not only reaps the fruit of his sublime discoveries, but becomes the sharer of his immortality.

Ros. Oh! may virtues and talents such as Frankenstein's, ever receive the patronage and protection of such men as the Prince del Piombino.

Prince. I rejoice that my dear Rosaura's admiration of this illustrious foreigner almost equals the enthusiasm of her brother's. Has her penetration ever hinted to her that last, that best, inestimable reward with which I meditate to crown my favours towards this Frankenstein? —

Ros. (Turning away) Ah, my brother! —

Prince. That blush, that downcast look, assure me that should my admiration of his merit induce me to confer on him a gift so precious as my sister's hand, I should not in her heart find an opposer of my generosity: — I will not tax your delicacy for a frank avowal, but in your silence read your acquiescence. this night, amidst the joyous mirth that fills our halls, will I hint to our philosopher, the dearer pleasure that I have in store for him.

Ros. My dear, dear brother! — A heart like yours will ever find the secret of making all around it happy.

[*Exeunt into Palace.*

SCENE II.

A Nearer View of the Outside of the Pavilion, appropriated as Frankenstein's study; practicable door, and transparent window above. (dark.)

Enter Frankenstein, from the Pavilion.

Fran. It comes — it comes! — 'tis nigh — the moment that shall crown my patient labours, that shall gild my toilsome studies with the brightest joy that e'er was yet attained by mortal man. — What monarch's power what general's valour, or what hero's fame, can rank with that of Frankenstein? What can their choicest efforts accomplish, but to destroy? 'Tis mine, mine only to create, to breathe the breath of life into a mass of putrifying mortality; 'tis mine to call into existence a form conceived in my own notions of perfection! How vain, how worthless, is the noblest fame compared to mine! — Frankenstein shall be the first of men! — And this triumph is at hand; but a few moments and it is accomplished! Burst not, high swelling heart, with this o'erwhelming tide of joy!

Enter Julio, O.P.

7

Ju. Ah! my dear sir, I have not seen you before, today; I am so glad to meet with you.

Fran. (Abstractedly) 'Tis well, boy. — Good even to you.

Ju. There are such doings in the palace; such feastings, and such merry–makings, and all, as they say, for you.

Fran. Why that is better; 'tis as it should be. Doubt not, I will be with ye. Let the full bowl high sparkle, let the joyous note swell loud; I will be there, exulting in my triumph.

Ju. Aye, but moreover than all that, I could — but I don't think I shall, because it was told to me as a very great secret — I could tell you of something that would make you so happy.

Fran. I shall, I must be happy; the secret is my own. Leave me, boy, leave me.

Ju. Nay, now, you do not love your poor Julio; I'm sure I know not how I have offended you; but you never spoke to me thus harshly before.

Fran. (embraces him) Nay, my pretty pupil, my affectionate Julio, I must love thee, ever. I am disturbed by intense study, and for a few moments I would be alone.

Ju. If you are sure you love me, I will leave you; but if I had offended you, I would not leave you till you had forgiven me, I would not, indeed; we shall see you anon. I shall know where to find you, by my pretty aunt Rosaura's side. Oh, if you did but know what I could tell you!

[*He runs off. O.P.*

Fran. The time is come, the glorious moment is arriv'd. Now, Frankenstein, achieve the mighty work, gain that best of victories, a victory o'er the grave!

[*Exit into the Pavilion.*

Enter STRUTT, *with a ladder,– and* LISETTA.

FRANKENSTEIN; OR, THE MAN AND THE MONSTER!

Strutt. Well now, do you know, Lisetta, I'm going to do a great deal more for you, than I dare to do for myself. I'm dying to know what my master is about yonder, but if he should catch me peeping, what a jolly thump o' the head I shall get, to be sure; and then, Lisetta, you have it in your power to break my heart, and that's a great deal worse.

Lis. Well, now, without any more ado, you put the ladder against the window, and hold it fast, whilst I mount up and see what he is about.

Strutt. Fie, for shame, Lisetta, what are you thinking about! I'll get up the ladder, and I'll report all that I see, to you below.

Lis. Well, just as you please, only I'd rather peep myself, because, you know, seeing is believing. *(Strutt places the Ladder against the window of the Pavilion, mounts it, and peeps in; a faint glimmering of light is seen through the window.)* Well, now, what can you see?

Strutt. Why, I can see a little fire, and a great deal of smoke.

Lis. And I suppose all your boasted discoveries will end in smoke.

Strutt. Oh! now I can see better; — and would you believe it, Lisetta, from all I can see, I really do think, at least it seems so to me, that my master is making a man.

Lis. Making a man! — What, is not he alone?

Strutt. Yes, quite alone. *(A strong and sudden flash of light is now seen at the window; Strutt slides down the Ladder.)* Oh, Lord! that's too much for me! — he's raising the devil — he's blown off the top of the pavilion! — Run, run, Lisetta, or the old gentleman will have you!

Lis. Nay, then the devil take the hindmost, I say!

[They run off. O. P.

SCENE III.

The Interior of the Pavilion. — Folding Doors in the Back. On a long Table is discovered an indistinct form, covered with a black cloth. A small side Table, with Bottles, and Chemical Apparatus, — and a brazier with fire.

FRANKENSTEIN is discovered, as if engaged in a calculation.

Fran. Now that the final operation is accomplished, my panting heart dares scarcely gaze upon the object of its labours — dares scarcely contemplate the grand fulfilment of its wishes. Courage, Frankenstein! glut thy big soul with exultation! — enjoy a triumph never yet attained by mortal man! *(music. — He eagerly lays his hand on the bosom of the figure, as if to discover whether it breathes.)* The breath of life now swells its bosom. — *(Music.)* As the cool night breeze plays upon its brow, it will awake to sense and motion. *(Music. — He rolls back the black covering, which discovers a colossal human figure, of a cadaverous livid complexion; it slowly begins to rise, gradually attaining an erect posture,* Frankenstein *observing with intense anxiety. When it has attained a perpendicular position, and glares its eyes upon him, he starts back with horror.)* Merciful Heaven! And has the fondest visions of my fancy awakened to this terrible reality; a form of horror, which I scarcely dare to look upon: — instead of the fresh colour of humanity, he wears the livid hue of the damp grave. Oh, horror! horror! — let me fly this dreadful monster of my own creation! *(He hides his face in his hands; the* Monster, *meantime, springs from the table, and gradually gains the use of his limbs; he is surprized at the appearance of* Frankenstein, — *advances towards him and touches him; the latter starts back in disgust and horror, draws his sword and rushes on the* Monster, *who with the utmost care takes the sword from him, snaps it in two, and throws it down.* Frankenstein *then attempts to seize it by the throat, but by a very slight exertion of its powers, it throws him off to a considerable distance; in shame, confusion, and despair,* Frankenstein *rushes out of the Apartment, locking the doors after him. The* Monster *gazes about it in wonder, traverses the Apartment; hearing the sound of* Frankenstein's *footsteps without, wishes to follow him; finds the opposition of the door, with one blow strikes it from its hinges, and rushes out.)*

SCENE IV.

Outside of the Pavilion, as before.
Frankenstein, *in great agitation, rushes from the Pavilion locking the door after him.*

Fran. (After a pause of much terror.) Have all my dreams of greatness ended here? Is this the boasted wonder of my science, — is this the offspring of long years of toilsome study and noisome labour? Is my fairest model of perfection come to this — a hideous monster, a loathsome mass of animated putrefaction, whom, but to gaze on chills with horror even me, his maker? How, how shall I secrete him, how destroy? Heaven! to think that in the very moment of fruition, when all my toils were ended and I should glory in their noble consummation, my first, my dearest, only wish, is to annihilate what I have made! Horrible object, wretched produce of my ill−directed efforts! never must thou meet another eye than mine — never must thou gaze upon a human being, whom thy fell aspect sure would kill with terror! *(A tremendous crash is heard, the Monster breaks through the door of the Pavilion)* Ah! he is here! I have endued him with a giant's strength, and he will use it to pluck down ruin on his maker's head. *(Music. — The Monster approaches him with gestures of conciliation.)* — Hence! avoid me! do not approach me, wretch! thy horrid contact would spread a pestilence throughout my veins; touch me, and I will straightway strike thee back to nothingness! *The* Monster *still approaches him with friendly gestures —* Frankenstein *endeavours to stab him with his dagger, which the* Monster *strikes from his hand; — whilst the* Monster *is taking up the dagger, and admiring its form,* Frankenstein *steals off. — The* Monster, *perceiving him gone, rushes off, as if in pursuit, but in an opposite direction.*

SCENE V.

The heart of a gloomy and intricate Forest. — Tremendous Storm, Thunder, Lightning, Rain,

Enter RITZBERG, — *and* EMMELINE *bearing the Child.*

Em. The thunder's awful voice, and the fierce tumult of the wildly raging storm, have drowned thy plaintive wailings, my poor babe, and thou art hushed to silence. Sleep on, my babe, let thy mother's throbbing bosom shelter thee. We shall find him soon, — yes, I am sure we shall. — And when he sees thy ruddy smiling cheek, and marks his Emmeline's wan and haggard features, his heart will turn to us, he will again be all our own.

Ritz. I don't believe a word of it. Talk of his heart, indeed! he has no heart: if ever he had any, it has evaporated in the fumes of his diabolical preparations. He love and protect you! all his affections are in the bottom of a crucible; and in the wild chimeras of his science, and the dreams of his mad ambition, all his human feelings are lost and annihilated.

Em. Oh, no! my father; the enthusiasm of knowledge, the applauses of the powerful, may for a time, have weaned him from us but my own kind, gentle, Frankenstein, can never be inhuman.

Ritz. Can't he? Well, I don't know what you may call it; but to deceive and trepan a young, innocent confiding creature, as you were, and to leave you and your child to poverty and want, whilst he went rambling in the train of a prince, after his own devilish devices;— if that is not inhuman, I don't know what is.

Em. Ah, my father; I have heard that the Prince del Piombino has an estate in this beautiful island; that he has, attached to his household, a wonderful philosopher — I am confident 'tis he — and oh! my heart tells me, that he will shortly bless us with his returning love.

Ritz. Yes, and with this fine tale, and because I could not bear to see you pining away in hopeless sorrow, have you lured me to quit my quiet, peaceful abode in Germany, and come wandering over here to Sicily. And today you must march out on a pretty wild–goose chase, to endeavour to trace him in the household of this prince; till we have lost our way in the mazes of this forest, and can't trace a path back again to the hovel I have hired. And it's my belief, that if you found him in the Prince's palace, you would be driven away from the gate like a common beggar.

Em. Oh, say not so, my father; do not destroy my hope, for in that consists the little strength that now remains to me.

(Storm rages furiously.)

12

Ritz. And a pretty night this for a young, delicate creature like you, with your helpless infant, to be out in. — Curses, a thousand curses on the villain — !

Em. Oh, no, my father, no! — Do not curse him. Curse not the husband of your Emmeline — the father of her child!

Ritz. Well, well, I won't — the damn'd good–for–nothing vagabond! — I dare'nt stir a step in this plaguy forest, for all the storm keeps such a beautiful hubbub about us, for fear of straying further out of the way; and I am sure you have no strength to waste. — But here, I have it. You stay here, exactly where I leave you; give me the child, for you must be tired of carrying it, and I'll endeavour to find the path. — when I have traced it, I'll return for you. — There, stay here, just under this tree; it will afford a partial shelter. I warrant me, that with the assistance of the lightning, which keeps flashing so merrily, I shall soon discover the path. — I think I've got an inkling of it now. *(Takes the* Child *from* Emmeline, *and goes out as if endeavouring to trace the path. U. E. P. S.)*

Em. My spirits fail me, and my strength is exhausted. Whilst I bore the child, nature gave me powers, and I could not sink beneath the grateful burden. — Ah what a peal was there! — Heaven itself joins in the persecution of the hapless Emmeline. — Father, father! come to me! — I sink — I die — oh, Frankenstein! Frankenstein! *(She falls on the ground — the storm still continues to rage. The* Monster *enters in alarm and wonder, stares wildly about him; at length perceives* Emmeline *extended on the ground — is struck with wonder, approaches and raises her; is filled with admiration; expresses that the rain occasions inconvenience, and that the lightning is dreadful, his pity for* Emmeline *being exposed to it, his wish to procure her shelter; at length takes her up in his arms, and bears her off.)*

Re–enter RITZBERG, *with the* Child.

Ritz: Come, Emmeline, I think I have found it at last, and we shall be snug at home before the thunder can give another growl at us. — *(Perceives that she is gone.)* Merciful Heaven! not here! Where can she be gone? Surely no danger can have approached her. — She has wandered on, endeavouring to overtake me, and has mistaken the path, and so increased our troubles. Imprudent girl! — Emmeline, my child, my girl, my Emmeline

[*Exit with the Child, calling aloud.*

SCENE VI.

The Inside of Ritzberg's Cottage. — Entrance Door in Flat; in some part of the Scene, a Fire–place.

(The Monster *dashes open the door, and enters, bearing* Emmeline; *he places her in a chair, and looks round for some means of assisting her; perceives the fire, discovers by touching it, that it yields heat; removes the chair with* Emmeline, *to the fire, and remains watching her. The* Child *enters, on perceiving the* Monster *utters a shriek of terror, and runs across the stage, exclaiming,* 'Mother! –mother!' — Ritzberg *then enters, is likewise alarmed at the appearance of the* Monster. *The* Monster *observes the* Child *with admiration and beckons it to approach him which the* Child *refuses to do; he then softly approaches the* Child *with gestures of conciliation, the* Child *endeavouring to escape from him.* Emmeline *utters a piercing shriek —* Ritzberg *snatches up his gun, fires at the* Monster, *wounds it in the shoulder. The* Monster *puts down the* Child, *who rushes to his mother's embrace; expresses the agony occasioned by the wound; the rage inspired by the pain! would rush on* Ritzberg, *who keeps the gun presented; it is deterred by fear of a repetition of the wound; rushes out of the hut;* Ritzberg *remaining on the defensive; whilst* Emmeline *thanks Heaven for the preservation of her child.*

SCENE VII.

A Landscape.
Enter JULIO.

Ju. I can't conceive what has happened to Mr. Frankenstein; when I spoke to him this evening, he was so cross, and so abstracted, and so mysterious; and now here my father, the Prince, has given a grand festival, expressly to do him honour, and he is no where to be found. I wish I could meet with him. I think he loves me, and I would coax him out of his gloomy humour, and lead him smiling and good–natured to my aunt Rosaura or I'd know the reason why, I am determined. (*Music. — The* Monster *furiously rushes on.*) Ah! what dreadful gigantic creature is this? (*The* Monster *approaches and seizes him.*) Oh! — help, — mercy, — spare me, — spare me!— (*The Monster expresses that his kindly feelings towards the human race have been met by scorn, abhorrence, and violence, that*

14

they are all now converted into hate and vengeance; that Julio *shall be his first victim. He snatches him up and bears him off,* Julio *crying* 'Mercy! — help! help!'

SCENE VIII.

Splendid Banqueting Hall in the Palace, open in the back upon the Garden, and giving a View of the Lake. Banqueting Tables,

The

PRINCE *and* ROSAURA *discovered, on a Throne under the centre Arch. Company of both sexes,* Attendants, *A BALLET is performed, after which the Prince and Rosaura advance.*

Prince. I know not why it, that he in whose honour this entertainment was expressly given, should so long absent himself from our revels. Surely, for one night he might have relaxed from his deep studies.

Ros. I think he scarce will tarry longer, for I have sent Julio in search of him. — Ah! he is here.

Enter Frankenstein *in great agitation.*

Prince. At length you are arrived. Be assured, my friend, your absence has been both felt and regretted.

Fran. Accept my humble and sincere apology. I was engaged, most intently engaged, in the solution of a problem, on the result of which I had much at stake. *(aside)* My every hope depended on it, and the solution has stamped me a wretch for ever!

Prince. A truce to study, now, and moody thoughts. — Let the grape's sparkling juice chase from your brain all dark chimeras; partake the joy that smiles around you:— anon, I have a proposal to make to you, that will not damp your mirth, I trust.

Fran. Aye, let me be joyous; let me seek joy even at the bottom of the maddening bowl; I

15

cannot find it in my own heart. — Give me wine; — quick, let me drain a flowing goblet, perchance it may chase — oh! no, no, it can never drive from my remembrance that form of horror that exceeds conception.

Ros. From my hand will the cup bring less of joy? — Dear Frankenstein — I would say, learned sir, what means the dreadful wildness that gleams on your countenance?

Fran. Dear and most lovely lady, 'tis the intoxication of high swelling mirth of gratitude, of animating hilarity. Fair lady, permit the humblest of your slaves to pledge you. *(He is raising the cup to his lips, when* Quadro *hastily rushes in.*

Quad. Oh, my lord, my lord! — such intelligence of horror! — the young prince, Julio, has been murdered!

Fran. (Dashing the cup from him.) Eternal Heaven! — that fiend has perpetrated it!

Ros. Julio murdered!

Prince. My boy! my pretty, innocent, affectionate boy! say where, how, by whom?

Quad. He was found in the pavilion where Mr. Frankenstein pursues his studies, the door thrown from its hinges: from the mark on his neck, he appears to have been strangled.

Fran. (aside.) Then my worst fears have proved too true!

Prince. How could that lovely child provoke his fate? Robbery was not the object. Who could have the heart to harm that unoffending, darling child!

Quad. Can your highness doubt?

Prince. Speak, what mean you? On whom do your suspicions fall?

Quad. Who should it be, but this foreign adventurer, this Frankenstein?

Prince. Frankenstein!

FRANKENSTEIN; OR, THE MAN AND THE MONSTER!

Ros. Oh, Heavens!

Quad. Has any one else access to the pavilion, or ever presumes to enter it, or would have done now, except in eager search for the young prince?

Prince. I scarcely can believe it possible; but yet his lengthened absence from the festival at the very hour, his palpable agitation when he entered. — Frankenstein, what say you to this dreadful accusation?

Fran. I say that I am guilty, guilty a thousand times!

All. Ha!

Fran. Not of the crime of murder– I could not lay a finger in the way of violence on that lovely child. Mine is a guilt a thousand times more black, more horrible. I am the father of a thousand murders. Oh! presumption, and is this thy punishment? has my promised triumph brought me but to this?

Prince. Frankenstein! for mercy's sake explain. What horrid mystery lurks beneath thy words?

(Shots and noise of pursuit heard without — the Monster *rushes in through the archway in the back, pursued by* Peasants *variously armed — all shriek with horror — he rushes up to* Frankenstein, *and casts himself at his feet, imploring protection*)

Fran. Hated, detested fiend! now reeking with the blood of innocence — fiend of malice and destruction — here on thy hated head, I now invoke a father's and a prince's vengeance. Die, monster, die! and quit the life thou hast disgraced by blood and slaughter. — *(he seizes on the* Monster — *the guards close round — the* Monster *dashes* Frankenstein *to the earth, and by an exertion of his immense strength breaks through the opposing line — the* Prince *gives the word to fire — the* Monster, *snatching up the* Officer *holds him as a target before him — he receives the shots and falls dead — the* Monster *rushes up the steps of the throne and laughs exultingly — a general picture is formed, on which the Drop falls.)*

ACT II

SCENE I.

A Cellar belonging to the Villa, entered only by a ladder from a small Trap–door above.

Strutt. (discovered) Well, my master has done a nice job for himself, it should seem, with all his machinery and magic; the making of a man has rendered him a made man for life, and I seem destined to share all his advantages. Because his hopeful bantling chose to amuse itself with strangling a child, much in the same way, I suppose, that our ordinary brats do kittens, out of pure kindness, they have seized hold of me and popped me into this underground apartment, to keep me out of mischief; as if they thought I shared my master's propensities, and had a penchant for making of men and strangling of children. — And so, after having taught me philosophy, my master has left me here to practise it. Now, if this were a wine cellar, there would be some kind of consolation; I might, by the magic of a butt of good liquor, convert this dungeon into a fairy palace, and when I could stand no longer, fancy these hard stones were silken cushions. But every thing now has the appearance of a cursed uncomfortable reality. Ha! I think I hear some one coming. I suppose it's old Quadro, who is about to set me at liberty, or at least to afford me the consolation of a flaggon of his best. *(The trap–door above opens, a ladder is put down, and* Quadro *descends followed by* Lisetta.) Ah! how d'ye do; I'm so glad to see you. I hope you are come to bring me comfort in one shape or the other.

Quad. Oh, yes! the best of all possible comfort, the news of a speedy termination to all your miseries; you will very shortly be exalted, my fine fellow, elevated, tucked up, dance upon nothing.

Strutt. Don't mention it. I assure you such allusions are altogether unpleasant to my feelings; for though you may consider my master a bit of a mountebank, I assure you that I have never been accustomed to dance on a tight rope; and as to hanging — *(to* Lisette) oh! you dear little creature, I have dreamt of nothing but hanging round your neck — whilst for tucking up, I had hoped we should have been both tucked up together in the bridal bed, before this.

FRANKENSTEIN; OR, THE MAN AND THE MONSTER!

Lis. Oh! for shame, sir!

Quad. Oh! you did, did you? I can tell you that there is a very narrow bed in preparation for you, where you will find it most convenient to lie alone, and where you will be tucked up with the sexton's shovel.

Strutt. I am surprised at your mentioning such indelicacies before a young lady.

Quad. In the confusion occasioned by the appearance of his delectable companion, your pretty master effected his escape; but I took care to grapple you. I considered the nabbing of such a fellow as you to be in my department, and so I popped you into this cellar.

Strutt. It would have been much more handsome of you to pop me in the cellar where you keep the liquor.

Quad. And you will be hanged for having aided, abetted, and assisted your master in the formation of a monster, and as an accessory in the young Prince's murder.

Strutt. Signor Quadro, you shock me. Me accused of assisting to make a man! Let me tell you I was never before suspected of such an offence; not even by the beadle of our parish, and he was a sharp chap at nosing out such matters, I warrant ye.

Quad. But now, sir, you are in my clutches, you won't get off so easy you may depend on it.

Strutt. Oh, Mr. Frankenstein! Mr. Frankenstein! this is a pretty mess you have got me into, to stand god–father to your monster. — *(he sits down in the back)*

Lis. Now, my dear father, how can you be so harsh to this poor young man? I don't really believe he had any hand in it; in my opinion, he would not be concerned in the making of any thing half so ugly.

Quad. Did not I say it from the beginning; did not I always insist that they were a brace of vagabonds, and that no good would come of harbouring them?

Lis. But now my own good, kind, dear father, seeing that what is done cannot be undone, and that hanging this young man would only make bad worse, could not you contrive to let him go?

Quad. Let him go, indeed! and what for?

Lis. Why just to oblige me, father; for really he is a tolerably well–behaved young man enough, and not so much amiss to look at.

Quad. Oh! you think so? And then, I suppose, the next thing is that you must go with him, eh, you minx? Go and see him hanged if you like.

Lis. Now my dear beautiful father, you don't know, though you are rather old, how well you look when you are doing a good–natured action. *(She makes signs behind his back to* Strutt, *to take advantage of the opportunity and run up the ladder.)*

Quad. You coaxing Jezebel! But don't think to wheedle me out of my duty.

Lis. Now look in my face. *(places one hand on each side of his face, as if to turn it towards her;* Strutt *watches his opportunity and silently ascends the ladder)* Look in my face, and frown a refusal if you can. Will you let him go?

Quad. No, I won't.

Lis. You are sure you won't?

Quad. No, I'll be damned if I do. (Strutt *has now gained the top of the ladder.)*

Lis. Then I'd advise him to do as I shall, to be off without asking your leave, and let you enjoy the comforts of this place by yourself. *(She runs to the ladder, and with* Strutt's *assistance hastily ascends it, after which they quickly draw up the ladder.)*

Quad. Why, you jade, you vixen, you undutiful hussey, what do you mean?

Lis. Only to let you stay there, father, till the young man is out of your reach; for I could not bear that you should have his death upon your conscience, father, I could not, indeed.

Quad. Go, both of you, and people the world with monsters, if you will; you can produce none worse than an unnatural daughter.

Strutt. Good bye, old gentleman!

Strutt *and* Lisetta *disappear with the ladder,* Quadro *rushes out with a rage on the opposite side.)*

SCENE II.

The inside of Ritzberg's Cottage, as before.

Frankenstein *rushes in, in great agitation.*

Fran. Where am I? Let me a moment pause, collect my distracted thoughts — compose, if possible, this tumult of the brain. I have fled! and wherefore fled? Had not death been welcome? But then to perish on a scaffold — loaded with infamy — branded with a crime my very soul abhors — the murder of an innocent I would have died to save. No, no, it must not be — not yet. My life has been devoted to the fulfilment of one object, another now claims the exertion of its short remainder, to destroy the wretch that I have formed — to purge the world of that infuriated monster — to free mankind from the fell persecution of that demon. This, this is now my bounden duty, and to this awful task I solemnly devote myself.

Enter EMMELINE *and* Child

Em. A stranger here! Ah! can I believe my senses — am I indeed so blest, does he come to seek his Emmeline? My lord, my life, my Frankenstein!

Fran. What do I behold? Emmeline Ritzberg! Lost, guilty, cursed wretch! thy cup of crime and misery is full. Hell yawns for thee, and all thy victims now surround thee, calling down Heaven's vengeance on thy head.

Em. And is it thus? Is Emmeline's presence, then, a curse? Farewell, then, hope. — But we'll not persecute thee, Frankenstein, for with my child I'll wander where thou shalt

21

never more be punished with remembrance of us, and where death will soon end our sorrow.

Fran. Emmeline! Emmeline! tear not my heart with words like those. What to a guilty wretch can be a greater curse than the presence of those he has injured? Now at thy feet behold me, Emmeline, in humble agony of heart, I plead for thy forgiveness. Oh! that I ne'er had quitted thy peaceful blest abode — ne'er let into my bosom those demons of ambition and fell pride, that now, with ceaseless gnawing, prey upon my soul.

Em. Not at my feet, but in my arms, dear Frankenstein, lose all the memory of sorrows past. Oh! if thy heart still owns thy Emmeline, all shall be well, be happy — One fond embrace of thine repays an age of sorrow; in thy smiles and those of this sweet cherub, I shall again awake to joy.

Fran. Oh Emmeline, since we parted, all has been crime; crime of so black a dye, that even to thy gentle forgiving spirit, I dare not confess it. Crime, whose punishment will be unceasing, will be eternal.

Em. Oh, no, my Frankenstein, guilt, to be absolved needs but to be abjured. Returned to virtue and domestic peace, thy Emmeline shall soothe thy every woe, and on her bosom thou'lt forget thy griefs.

Fran. I dare not hope it. But in this land I cannot hope a moment's ease. Quick, let us fly — far, far from this accursed spot, the bane of all my peace. There, to that calm retreat, where first thy angel charms awoke my soul to love, there let us quick repair. Oh, that in former and in happier scenes, I could forget the guilt, the misery that I have since been slave to.

Enter hastily RITZBERG, *Door in Flat*

Ritz. Ha! Frankenstein here! but 'tis no time to parley; the cottage is on fire! That fierce gigantic figure of terrific aspect, waves aloft his torch, as if in triumph at the deed. *(a coarse yelling laugh is heard.)*

Fran. Ha! 'tis that hideous voice! Quick, quick, let us fly! His hellish malice still pursues me, and but with his death or with mine, will this fierce persecution cease. Could I but

22

place you beyond his power! *(With Ritzberg he attempts to open the door, they find it barricaded from without; the laugh is repeated — the conflagration has enveloped the whole building — Frankenstein rushes off as if in search of some other outlet — Part of the building breaks — The Monster enters at the chasm, seizes on Emmeline and the Child, and bears them through the burning ruins, followed by Ritzberg. Frankenstein returns, perceives that Emmeline and her Child are gone, and in despair rushes after them.)*

SCENE III.

A Landscape.

Enter STRUTT *and* LISETTA. (P.S.)

Strutt. Well, Lisetta, and now having by your assistance escaped from the clutches of that cantankerous old father of yours. What is next to be done?

Lis. Why as I have got out of his clutches at the same time, and so lost my natural protector, what do you think you ought to do next?

Strutt. Why, I suppose you think I ought to marry you?

Lis. Whilst you, perhaps, are of a very different opinion.

Strutt. Not in the least, my angel; but then my poor master, he perhaps is in trouble, and requires my assistance; and to desert him in the hour of need, I could not do it, Lisetta, no, not to possess such a treasure as yourself.

Lis. And if you could I should despise you for it. But suppose, Mr. Strutt, we were both to go and assist him. Two heads, they say, are better than one, and so are two pair of hands: and instead of having one faithful follower he would have a couple, that's all.

Strutt. What, no, you don't mean it, do you? Will you really take me for better for worse, and go with me in search of my poor dear master? Well, I always thought you were a good creature, but now you're a perfect divinity, and I'll adore you.

Lis. Who knows, perhaps Mr. Frankenstein may get married too, and then he'll have better employment than making monsters.

Strutt. Oh, that monster! don't mention him, Lisetta. If he should be with my master now, do you think you would have the courage to face him? I'm not quite sure that I should.

Lis. Oh! never doubt me, if I take him in hand, I'll bring him to his senses, I warrant me; for if a spirited woman can't tame him, he must be a very fierce ungovernable devil indeed. — *(a scream is heard without.)*

Strutt. Ah! what means that shriek? See, yonder where the demon comes, he bears with him both a woman and a child. She does not seem to have made much of a hand of him, at any rate. Here, back, back, conceal yourself, Lisetta, I would not have him come within arm's length of you, for the world. *(he pulls her behind a tree.)*

(The Monster *enters, exultingly bearing* Emmeline *and her* Child, *crosses and exit.* Frankenstein *follows him with a staggering step, almost overcome with fatigue and terror.* (P.S.) *to* (O.P.)

Strutt. (coming from his concealment.) What, ho! Sir! master! Mr. Frankenstein! 'Tis Strutt, your faithful servant! He hears me not, but madly still pursues the fiend he cannot hope to master.

Lis. And will you, too, Strutt, be mad enough to follow him?

Strutt. Why, not singly, because I think it would be to little purpose; but I'll tell you what I'll do — I'll first bestow you in a place of safety, and then I'll summon together a few stout–hearted fellows, and we'll see if we can't settle his monstership; for sooner than he should harm that poor woman and her infant, damme, he shall kill and eat me — but I'll endeavour to give him a belly full.

[*Exeunt* (O.P.)

SCENE IV.

A tremendous range of craggy precipices, near the summit of Mount Etna. On the P.S. *a conspicuous pillar of rock stands on a lofty elevation. The only approach is from the depths below.*

(The Monster, *with gigantic strides, ascends from below with* Emmeline *and the* Child — *she is so overcome with fatigue and terror as to be unable to speak — the* Monster *gains the elevation, and with a cord that is round his waist, binds* Emmeline *to the pillar of rock — He returns to the* Child — Emmeline *sinks on her knees in supplication —* Frankenstein *with great difficulty ascends from below — he perceives his* Child *in the* Monster's *power — he is about to rush on him; the* Monster *defies him — and* Frankenstein, *recollecting his former defeats, abandons his threatening gestures and assumes one of entreaty.)*

Fran. Demon of cruelty, art thou still insatiate with the blood of innocence? how many victims does it require to content thy rage? I do implore thee, I, thy creator, who gave thee life, who endued thee with that matchless strength I cannot hope to master, I, on my knees, entreat thee but to spare that innocent. If fury and the thirst of blood be in thy hellish nature, on me, on me glut thy fell appetite — but, oh! if in thy human frame there dwells one spark of human sympathy or feeling, spare, spare, that unoffending child.

(The monster points to his wound — expresses that he would willingly have served Frankenstein *and befriended him, but that all his overtures were repelled with scorn and abhorrence — then, with malignant exultation siezes on the* Child, *and whirls it aloft, as if about to dash it down the rock —* Emmeline *screams,* Frankenstein, *with a cry of horror, covers his eyes — at this moment a thought occurs to* Emmeline — *she pulls from under her dress a small flagelot, and begins to play an air — its effect on the* Monster *is instantaneous — he is at once astonished and delighted — he places the* Child *on the ground — his feelings become more powerfully affected by the music, and his attention absorbed by it — the* Child *escapes to its father —* Emmeline *continues to play, and* Frankenstein *intently to watch its effect on the* Monster. *As the air proceeds his feelings become more powerfully excited — he is moved to tears; afterwards, on the music assuming a lively character, he is worked up to a paroxysm of delight — and on its again becoming mournful, is quite subdued, till he lays down exhausted at the foot of the rock to which* Emmeline *is attached.)*

(Strutt *now rushes on with* Ritzberg *and a number of* Peasants *variously armed, and furnished with strong cords.)*

Strutt. There he is! that's him! That's my gentleman! and luckily for us, he seems to be in a bit of a snooze — now's our time or never. On him my lads, and bind him fast, and then we shall be all right.

(With Ritzberg *and others, he immediately falls on the* Monster *and they bind him stoutly with cords* — Frankenstein *has meantime released* Emmeline — *the* Monster *makes prodigious exertions of strength to burst his bonds, but he is overpowered by the number of his adversaries.)*

Strutt. Away, away, sir, and place the lady and child in safety. I'll take care and accomodate this gentleman with snug quarters, and return immediately to attend your commands.

Fran. Faithful creature! Eternal Providence, receive my thanks; and if it be thy pleasure to inflict on me an added punishment, oh! on this guilty head alone direct thy wrath; spare those who are most dear to me, those whose innocence may challenge thy compassion! (With Emmeline and the Child he commences the descent, and disappears.)

Strutt. Now I think the best thing we can do is to fasten my gentleman to this pinnacle of rock; the cool air of this exalted region may give him an appetite; but he will stand very little chance of getting it gratified, unless the lava should flow from the volcano, and that may be a kind of cordial for him *(They are binding him to the rock, the* Monster *making a furious resistance, in the course of which he hurls one of the* Peasants *to the depths below.)* — That's right, make a tight job of it, whilst you are about it; for if he once gets loose, he'll play the devil with you all; he'd crack you like so many walnuts. There, I think he'll do now; there's not much fear of his troubling us again for one while. If he gets away from here, and finds his way down to terra firma again, I'll give him leave to drink hob–and–nob with me, in the cup I have filled to celebrate his overthrow.

(They descend the precipice by means of ropes and ladders, leaving the Monster *attached to the pinnacle of rock — when they are gone, he redoubles his efforts to escape from his bonds, and at length succeeds — he surveys the chasm, and is afraid to venture down it— he firmly attaches to the pinnacle one end of the cord by which he was bound — and by means of this lowers himself down the chasm)*

SCENE V.

A Subterranean Passage hollowed in the Mountain.

Enter STRUTT *and* Peasants, *(P.S.)*

Strutt. Faith, my lads, it's cold work this, climbing so near the summit of Etna, in a chill evening breeze — yes, and fatiguing work too — catching such game as we've been after is no boy's play. Lord, what a chap my master must be, to be sure, when he was making a man — he thought he might as well have a wapper at once, I suppose. Now I say, a little and good for my money. But, however, we have quieted my gentleman, and I think we have done a much better job than my master did in making him. And now I can tell you a secret. This passage leads to the hermitage of father Antonio; that you all know, so that's no secret; but what you perhaps do not know is, that old Quadro, the Prince's butler, whenever he visits the holy father to confess, always brings a bottle or two of prime old wine, which is employed by the hermit in lieu of penance; and so he makes his master pay for all his sins, and purchases absolution for one by committing another. Now do you know, I really think, that we better deserve this wine than the reverend father, and my proposal is that we adjourn to his cave and drink to the future prosperity of the heroes who subdued the monster.

[Shout, and exeunt, (O.P.)

SCENE VI.

Interior of the Hermit's Cave.

STRUTT *and* Peasants *discovered seated round a table.*

Strutt. Well, upon my soul, it's a monstrous pleasant retreat. And now for the little store of choice Falernian.

Peas. (who has been hunting about the cave) Here it is, master Strutt; here's his reverence's holy water.

Strutt. Out with it, then, and in with it. If his reverence should miss it when he comes home, he knows where to get more. Old Quadro's sins will always keep his cellar well stocked. So now my lads, charge your cups — (Peasants *have meanwhile placed on the table several flaggons of wine, horns,* Now for it, fill all, and mind it's a bumper. (all fill) *Here's confusion to any creature that would harm a defenceless woman and a helpless child; for be their shape what it may, they must be monsters indeed.*

Peas. Bravo! with all my hert! *(all drink.)*

Strutt. And now I'll give you another. Here's our noble selves, and may all our future enterprizes be crowned with as complete success, as that which we have now so gloriously achieved.

(They have their cups raised to their lips, when the Monster, *still lowering himself by his rope, descends from an aperture in the roof of the cavern, and stands on the table in the midst of them — they all shrink back in terror with loud cries — the* Monster, *with one blow, dashes the table in pieces all fly in extreme fear — the* Monster *in rage dashes about the seats —* Strutt *takes an opportunity to stab him in the back, and flies leaving the dagger in the wound — the* Monster *extracts it, and roaring with pain rushes off.)*

SCENE VII.

A narrow rocky path–way, leading to the summit of Etna.

Enter STRUTT *and* Peasants *rapidly retreating from the* Monster — *the* Monster *follows in pursuit.* — Frankenstein *enters with* Emmeline — *they are followed by a party of* Soldiers, *whom* Frankenstein *encourages to the attack of the* Monster.

[*They all go off in pursuit, from* P.S. *to* O.P.

SCENE VIII

The Summit of Mount Etna — the Crater occupies the middle of the stage — near it is the Path–way from below — in very distant perspective are seen the sea and towns at the foot of Etna — the Volcano during the scene throws out torrents of fire, sparks, smoke, as at the commencement of an eruption.

(The Monster *ascends from below, faint from loss of blood and overcome by fatigue — he is followed by* Frankenstein, *whom he immediately attacks and stabs with the dagger he had taken from his wound — as* Frankenstein *falls,* Emmeline *rushes in shrieking and catches his lifeless body — the* Monster, *attempting to escape, is met at every outlet by armed* Peasantry *— in despair he rushes up to the apex of the mountain – the* Soldiery *rush in and fire on him — he immediately leaps into the Crater, now vomiting burning lava, and the curtain falls.)*

FINIS.

CPSIA information can be obtained at www.ICGtesting.com
Printed in the USA
LVOW051340261111

256447LV00003B/224/A